CAVE CRAWLERS

Pam Rosenberg

Raintree

Chicago, Illinois

www.capstonepub.com
Visit our website to find out
more information about
Heinemann-Raintree books.

To order:
☎ Phone 800-747-4992
🖥 Visit www.capstonepub.com
to browse our catalog and order online.

© 2012 Heinemann Library
an imprint of Capstone Global Library, LLC
Chicago, Illinois

Edited by Rebecca Rissman, Dan Nunn,
    and Sian Smith
Designed by Joanna Hinton Malivoire
Picture research by Elizabeth Alexander
Production by Victoria Fitzgerald
Originated by Capstone Global Library

**Library of Congress Cataloging-in-Publication
Data**
Rosenberg, Pam.
  Cave crawlers / Pam Rosenberg.
    p. cm.—(Landform adventurers)
  Includes bibliographical references and index.
  ISBN 978-1-4109-4137-4 (hb)
  ISBN 978-1-4109-4144-2 (pb)
1. Caves—Juvenile literature. I. Title.
  GB601.2.R67 2012
  551.44'7—dc22   2010050059

Acknowledgments
We would like to thank the following for permission to
reproduce photographs:
Alamy: Anthony Baker, cover, Bert de Ruiter, 10, Boomer
Jerritt, 4, David Sutherland, 6, Gavin Newman, 15, Ladi
Kirn, 19, Robbie Shone, 12, 24; Getty Images: Ashley
Cooper, 8, Christopher Hope-Fitch, 28, Danita Delimont/
Gallo Images, 25, Handout, 18, John Cancalosi, 17,
Juan Carlos Munoz, 20, Philippe Crochet, 5, Todd
Gipstein/National Geographic, 7; iStockphoto: Günay
Mutlu, 11 top; National Geographic Creative: STEPHEN
ALVAREZ, 14, 26; Science Source: Martin Bond, 29,
Pascal Goetgheluck, 21; Shutterstock: Christophe Testi,
11 bottom, Grigory Kubatyan, 13, 16, Sági Elemér, 22,
Songquan Deng, 27, Stephanie Coffman, 9

Every effort has been made to contact copyright holders
of material reproduced in this book. Any omissions will
be rectified in subsequent printings if notice is given to
the publisher.

Some words are shown in bold, **like this**. You can find
out what they mean by looking in the glossary.

Contents

Discovering Caves

Do you like climbing, swimming, and exploring? You could think about becoming a **spelunker**! A spelunker is someone who explores caves.

Caves are like pockets in Earth.
Some caves are just big enough for
a person to fit inside. Others stretch
underground for many miles.

rock

water

Caves form in different ways. Most caves are formed when rock is worn away by water.

Some caves are formed when **lava** flows from a **volcano**. The top layer hardens, while lava flows underneath. When the lava stops flowing, a cave is left under the top, hard layer.

This cave in Hawaii was formed by lava.

Cave Explorers

You have to be strong to be a **spelunker**. You must be ready to crawl through small openings or swim through ice-cold water. You might need to use ropes to climb steep rock walls. Are you ready for the challenge?

DANGER AHEAD!

Caves can be dangerous places. Never go **caving** alone. Make sure you have at least one adult with you when you go exploring.

Some people like **spelunking** so much that they make it their job. They combine science and **caving**. These people are called **speleologists**.

What do speleologists need?

Helmets

Lights

Warm clothing

Sturdy boots

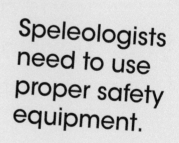

Speleologists need to use proper safety equipment.

Rocks and Water

Some **speleologists** explore caves to study rocks. If they are lucky, they might see **stalagmites** or **stalactites**! Speleologists use rock hammers and other tools to learn more about how caves formed.

Stalactite is spelled with a "c." Stalactites hang from the ceiling.

stalactite

stalagmite

Stalagmite is spelled with a "g." Stalagmites form on the ground.

Some caves are filled with water. These caves are dangerous! People need special training to explore them. They also need special tools such as air tanks and **fins**.

waterfall

Some caves even have waterfalls.

air tank

fin

Powerful lights are needed to explore underwater caves.

Who Lives in Caves?

Speleologists don't just study rocks. They study living things, too. During the day, bats hang from cave ceilings. They fly out when it gets dark. Nighttime is when they find insects to eat.

Carlsbad Caverns, New Mexico

CAVE FACT

Make sure you wear boots when you explore bat caves. The cave floor will be covered in **guano**, or bat poo! Guano is good for helping plants grow.

There are some animals that spend their whole lives in caves. They are blind. Can you guess why?

blind cave shrimp

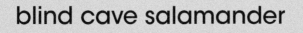

blind cave salamander

The answer is that they don't need to see, because it is too dark in caves! They use their other senses to get around.

Many people lived in caves thousands of years ago. How do we know this? **Speleologists** have found drawings and human **artifacts** in caves. Cameras are important tools for these cave explorers. They take pictures of the artifacts to study later.

CAVE FACT

Piles of **ancient** human poo can tell speleologists a lot about people who lived in caves many years ago. The poo can tell us what ancient people ate.

Amazing Caves

Caves can be found all over the world. Some are known for their size. Others have underground waterfalls or lakes. Some caves really *are* cool to explore—they are formed in ice!

Ice cave in Dobsina, Slovakia

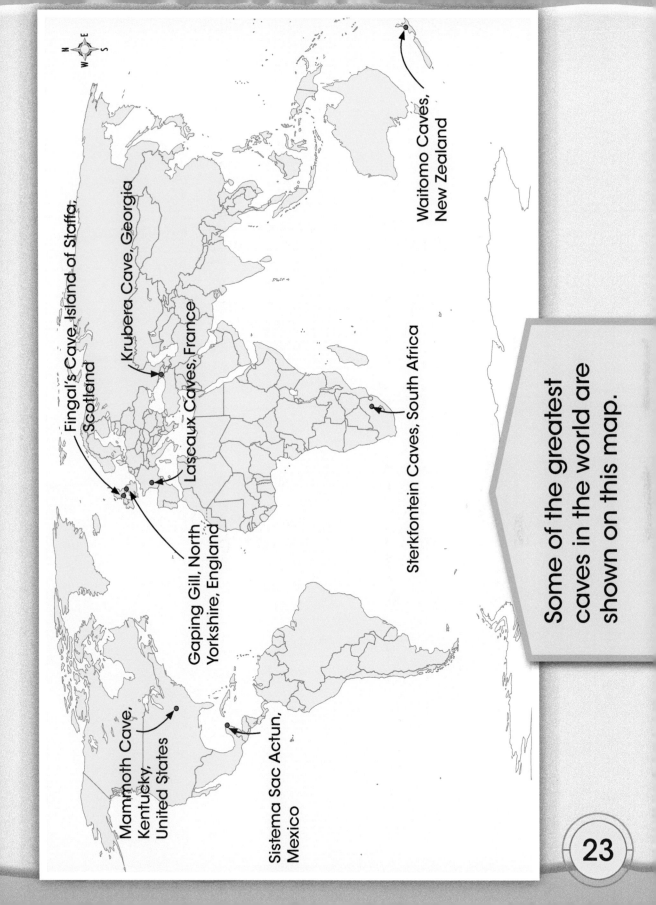

Fingal's Cave, Island of Staffa, Scotland

Krubera Cave, Georgia

Lascaux Caves, France

Gaping Gill, North Yorkshire, England

Waitomo Caves, New Zealand

Sterkfontein Caves, South Africa

Mammoth Cave, Kentucky, United States

Sistema Sac Actun, Mexico

Some of the greatest caves in the world are shown on this map.

Now That's Long!

Mammoth Cave, in Kentucky, is the world's longest known cave. More than 365 miles of passages have been explored. That is almost the length of the state of Illinois!

People visit Mammoth Cave
to see the amazing **stalactites**
and **stalagmites**.

Deep Underground

Krubera Cave is one of the world's deepest caves. It is found in the country of Georgia. The cave is over 7,000 feet deep. You could fit four Empire State Buildings in a hole that deep and still have room left over!

This climber is going down into Krubera Cave on a rope.

New York City

Empire State Building

Are You Ready to Explore?

Does being a cave crawler sound like fun to you? Then learn as much as you can about caves. Stay active, so that your body gets strong. Go swimming, hiking, and join a climbing club.

Ask your parents to help you find a group that explores caves in your area. Start exploring, and you may be a **speleologist** one day!

Glossary

ancient hundreds or thousands of years old

artifact object made or changed by humans

caving sport of exploring caves

fins long, flat rubber shoes that help divers to swim. Fins are also called "flippers."

guano bat or seabird poo

lava hot, liquid rock that comes out of a volcano when it erupts

speleologist scientist who studies and explores caves

spelunker person who explores caves as a hobby

spelunking sport of exploring caves

stalactite piece of rock shaped like an icicle that hangs from the ceiling of a cave

stalagmite piece of rock shaped like an icicle that sticks up from the floor of a cave

volcano vent in Earth's crust, or outer layer, through which lava, ash, and gas erupt

Find Out More

Find out

Which is the longest cave in the world?

Books

Cooper, Sharon Katz. *Horrible Habitats: Caves and Crevices*. Chicago: Raintree, 2010.

Gaff, Jackie. *I Wonder Why Stalactites Hang Down? and Other Questions About Caves*. Boston: Kingfisher, 2003.

Hutmacher, Kimberly. *Natural Wonders: Caves*. Mankato, Minn.: Capstone, 2011.

Websites

http://library.thinkquest.org/J0112123/
Find out about caves and some of the animals that might live there.

www.canyonsworldwide.com/crystals/index.html
Look inside a crystal cave using this website.

www.cave-exploring.com/Cave%20Types.htm
This website helps you learn about different kinds of caves and the basic rules of caving.

www.nps.gov/maca/forkids/index.htm
Learn about Mammoth Cave—and how kids can go caving there—at this website.

Index